The Rich Culture and History of Mongolia

DR. GAURAV GUPTA

PRABHAT
PRAKASHAN

Published by
PRABHAT PRAKASHAN PVT. LTD.
4/19 Asaf Ali Road,
New Delhi-110002 (INDIA)
e-mail: prabhatbooks@gmail.com

ISBN 978-93-5488-657-7
THE RICH CULTURE AND HISTORY OF MONGOLIA
by Dr. Gaurav Gupta

Edition
First, 2023

Price
₹ 200 (Rupees Two Hundred Only)

Printed at
Japan Art, Delhi

Author's Note

Mongolia is a land of vast landscapes, diverse cultures, and a rich history that spans back thousands of years. From the nomadic traditions of the Mongolian people to the conquests of Genghis Khan, this country has a unique and captivating story that deserves to be told.

The book "The rich culture and History of Mongolia" aims to provide a comprehensive look at the many facets of Mongolia, from its ancient history to its modernization and development. Each chapter delves into a specific aspect of Mongolian life and culture, providing readers with a deep understanding of this fascinating country.

Through the pages of this book, readers will learn about the customs and traditions of the Mongolian people, including their sports, food, music, and dance. They will also gain an appreciation for the beauty of Mongolia's natural landscapes, including its deserts, national parks, and wildlife reserves.

The book also explores Mongolia's political and economic evolution, from the days of the Mongol Empire to its current status as a developing nation with a growing mining industry. Readers will gain insights into the challenges and opportunities that Mongolia faces as it continues to modernize and expand its economy.

To ensure accuracy and depth of coverage, the book draws on a wide range of sources, including academic research, historical records, and firsthand accounts from Mongolian citizens and experts. We have strived to present a balanced and nuanced view of this complex country, while also conveying the unique spirit and character of the Mongolian people.

We hope that this book will serve as a valuable resource for anyone seeking to learn more about Mongolia, whether for academic, personal, or professional purposes. By providing a comprehensive and accessible overview of this remarkable country, we aim to inspire a greater appreciation for the beauty, history, and culture of Mongolia.

—Author

1.

Culture and Identity

Mongolia is a landlocked country located in East Asia, known for its unique and ancient culture. The Mongolian culture is deeply rooted in their nomadic way of life, which has been their traditional lifestyle for thousands of years. The Mongolian identity is closely linked to their culture, which includes their language, traditions, beliefs, and customs.

Language is an essential aspect of Mongolian culture and identity. Mongolian is the official language of Mongolia, and it is spoken by the majority of the population. The Mongolian language belongs to the Mongolic language family, which is a branch of the Altaic language family. The language has a rich history and is an integral part of the Mongolian culture. The Mongolian script, also known as the Uyghur script, is the traditional writing system used to write Mongolian. The script has been in use since the 12th century and is still used in Mongolia today.

Mongolian traditions and beliefs are deeply rooted in their nomadic lifestyle. The Mongolian people have a strong connection to the land, and their traditions reflect this. The traditional Mongolian dwelling is the yurt, which is a circular tent made of felt and wood. The yurt is easy to set up and take down, making it ideal for a nomadic lifestyle. Mongolian cuisine is also influenced by their nomadic lifestyle and includes meat dishes, such as mutton and beef, as well as dairy products, such as cheese and yogurt.

Mongolian music and dance are an integral part of their culture and identity. Mongolian traditional music is characterized by the use of the morin khuur, a two-stringed horsehead fiddle, and throat singing, also known as overtone singing. Throat singing is a unique style of singing where the singer can produce two or more notes simultaneously. Mongolian dance is also an important part of their culture and is often performed at festivals and celebrations. The traditional dances include the eagle dance, the camel dance, and the chopstick dance.

Religion is another important aspect of Mongolian culture and identity. The majority of Mongolians practice

Buddhism, which was introduced to Mongolia in the 16th century. Buddhism is deeply integrated into Mongolian culture and has influenced their art, architecture, and way of life. Shamanism is also practiced by some Mongolians, and it is believed to be the oldest religion in Mongolia. Shamanism involves communicating with spirits and ancestors through rituals and ceremonies.

❑

2.

Military Past

Mongolia is a country with a rich history of military conquests. From the time of Genghis Khan in the 13th century, the Mongolians have been known for their fierce warriors and their ability to conquer vast empires. In this chapter, we will explore Mongolia's military past and its legacy of conquest.

The Mongolian military was a formidable force that conquered much of Asia and Europe in the 13th and 14th centuries. The key to the Mongolian military's success was their use of cavalry and their ability to move quickly across vast distances. The Mongolian cavalry was known as the "horses of the sky," and they were highly skilled in horseback riding, archery, and sword fighting.

The Mongolian military was organized into units called tumens, each consisting of 10,000 soldiers. The tumens were further divided into smaller units called zuuns, each consisting of 1,000 soldiers. The Mongolian army was highly mobile and could cover vast distances in a short amount of time. This allowed them to surprise their enemies and launch unexpected attacks.

One of the most famous military leaders in Mongolian history was Genghis Khan. Genghis Khan was a brilliant strategist and a charismatic leader who united the various Mongolian tribes and launched a series of conquests that eventually led to the creation of the Mongol Empire. Genghis Khan's military campaigns were characterized by their brutality and their effectiveness. He conquered much of China, Central Asia, and Eastern Europe, and his empire eventually became the largest empire in history, spanning from China to Europe.

After Genghis Khan's death, his empire was divided among his sons and grandsons, who continued the tradition of conquest. One of his grandsons, Kublai Khan, established the Yuan Dynasty in China and became the first non-Chinese emperor to rule China. The Mongolian military was also instrumental in the defeat of the Islamic Khwarezmian Empire, which controlled much of Central Asia. The defeat of the Khwarezmian Empire paved the way for the Mongolian conquest of Persia and Eastern Europe.

The Mongolian military's success was due in large part to their use of innovative tactics and weapons. The Mongolian archers were particularly skilled and were able to fire arrows accurately while riding on horseback. The Mongolian military also made use of siege weapons such as trebuchets and catapults, which were used to break down walls and fortifications.

❑

3.

People and Their Traditions

Mongolian people and their traditions are a rich and diverse part of the country's cultural heritage. The traditions of the Mongolian people have been shaped by their nomadic lifestyle and their history of conquest and trade with neighboring countries.

The Mongolian people are known for their hospitality and their strong sense of community. One of the most important traditions in Mongolian culture is the concept of "ger" or "yurt," which is a traditional dwelling used by nomadic herders. The ger is a circular tent made of felt and canvas and is designed to be easily dismantled and transported. It is a symbol of the Mongolian nomadic lifestyle and is still used by many Mongolian families today.

The Mongolian people also have a rich tradition of music and dance. The "throat singing" or "khoomei" is a unique style of singing that involves creating multiple harmonic sounds simultaneously. This style of singing is often performed with traditional musical instruments such as the "morin khuur" or "horsehead fiddle." Mongolian folk dance is also an important part of the country's cultural heritage, with each region having its own unique style of dance.

Another important aspect of Mongolian culture is its cuisine. The nomadic lifestyle of the Mongolian people has influenced their cuisine, which consists of simple but hearty dishes that can be prepared quickly. The most famous Mongolian dish is "buuz," which is a type of steamed dumpling filled with meat and vegetables. Other popular dishes include "khuushuur," a fried pastry filled with meat, and "tsuivan," a noodle dish made with vegetables and meat.

The Mongolian people also have a long tradition of horsemanship and horse racing. Horse racing is a popular sport in Mongolia, and there are several festivals and events held throughout the year to celebrate it. The most famous of these events is the Naadam Festival, which takes place in July and features traditional sports such as horse racing, archery, and wrestling.

In addition to these traditions, the Mongolian people also have a strong spiritual connection to nature and their ancestors. Shamanism is an ancient tradition that is still practiced by many Mongolian families today. Shamanism involves the belief in spirits and the use of rituals to communicate with them. Mongolian Buddhism is also an important part of the country's spiritual heritage, with many Buddhist temples and monasteries located throughout the country.

❑

4.

Journey Through Mongolia

Mongolia is a vast country located in East Asia, known for its rugged terrain, nomadic culture, and rich history. A journey through Mongolia can be an unforgettable experience for any traveler seeking adventure, natural beauty, and cultural immersion. In this chapter, we will guide you through the essential aspects of exploring Mongolia as a tourist.

Firstly, when planning a trip to Mongolia, it is essential to understand the best time to visit. Mongolia has a continental climate with long, cold winters and short, hot summers. The best time to visit is during the summer months between June and August, when the weather is warm, and the landscapes are lush green. The Naadam festival, a traditional Mongolian festival featuring wrestling, horse racing, and archery, is held annually in

July, making it an excellent time to visit and experience Mongolian culture.

One of the most popular tourist destinations in Mongolia is the capital city, Ulaanbaatar. The city is a unique blend of modern and traditional, with a mix of Soviet-era buildings, traditional Mongolian architecture, and contemporary structures. Visitors can explore the Gandantegchinlen Monastery, the largest and most important Buddhist monastery in Mongolia, or visit the National Museum of Mongolia to learn about the country's history and culture.

Outside of the capital, Mongolia boasts vast expanses of untouched wilderness and natural beauty. The Gobi Desert, located in the south of the country, is one of the most popular tourist destinations. Visitors can ride camels across the dunes, explore ancient rock formations, and visit local nomadic families to learn about their way of life.

Another must-see destination in Mongolia is Lake Khuvsgul, one of the largest freshwater lakes in Asia. The crystal-clear waters and surrounding mountains make it a perfect spot for hiking, fishing, and kayaking. Visitors can also experience the Tsaatan people, a tribe of reindeer herders who inhabit the area.

The Orkhon Valley, located in central Mongolia, is a UNESCO World Heritage Site and is known for its historical significance. The valley was once the center of the Mongolian Empire and is home to many ancient ruins, including the Tuvkhun Monastery. Visitors can also enjoy horseback riding and hiking in the surrounding hills.

The Altai Mountains, are located in western Mongolia. The mountains are known for their stunning scenery and are home to several ethnic groups, including the Kazakhs and the Tuvans. Visitors can enjoy a variety of activities, including trekking, horseback riding, and bird-watching. The Altai Tavan Bogd National Park is a popular destination for tourists and is home to several glaciers and lakes.

When it comes to accommodation, Mongolia offers a range of options to suit different budgets and preferences. For those seeking an authentic Mongolian experience, staying in a traditional ger, a portable tent-like dwelling, is a must. Gers are used by nomadic families throughout Mongolia and provide a unique insight into the country's culture. For those seeking more luxury, there are several hotels and resorts located throughout the country.

One of the highlights of any trip to Mongolia is experiencing the country's rich culture and traditions. Mongolian cuisine is a unique blend of meat, dairy, and grains, with dishes such as buuz (steamed meat dumplings) and khuushuur (fried meat pies) being popular among locals and tourists alike. Visitors can also witness traditional Mongolian arts, such as throat singing, and attend cultural events such as Naadam.

❑

5.

Sports: Wrestling, Archery and Horse Racing

Sports are an integral part of Mongolian culture and traditions, with wrestling, archery, and horse racing being the most popular ones. In this chapter, we will discuss the history and significance of these sports in Mongolia.

Wrestling, or "Bokh," is the most popular sport in Mongolia. It has a long history, dating back to the time of the Mongol Empire. The sport is known for its unique rules, with no weight categories or time limits. The aim is to throw your opponent to the ground or force them out of the ring. The Naadam Festival, held annually in July, is the most important wrestling event in Mongolia. Thousands of wrestlers from across the country compete in this festival, which also includes archery and horse racing.

Archery, or "Tumen Ekh," is another popular sport in Mongolia. It has been a part of Mongolian culture for thousands of years and was once used as a military skill. The bows used in Mongolian archery are different from those used in other countries, with a unique design that allows for greater accuracy and distance. The aim is to hit a small target placed 75 meters away. The archery competition at the Naadam Festival is a must-see event, with archers dressed in traditional costumes and performing ceremonial rituals before the competition begins.

Horse racing, or "Urtyn Duu," is also an important part of Mongolian culture. It is a long-distance race, with horses covering a distance of 15 to 30 kilometers. The horses used in Mongolian horse racing are small but sturdy, bred for their stamina and endurance. The jockeys, usually young children, are trained in horse riding and are selected based on their weight. The Naadam Festival features some of the most exciting horse races, with horses and jockeys from across the country competing for the top prize.

In addition to these three sports, Mongolians also enjoy other traditional sports such as archery on horseback, falconry, and knucklebone shooting. These sports are often practiced during the winter months when outdoor activities are limited.

❑

6.

Mongolian Nomads

Mongolian Nomads are a unique and integral part of Mongolia's history, culture, and way of life. In this chapter, we will discuss the lifestyle and traditions of Mongolian nomads and their significance in modern-day Mongolia.

Nomadic life has been a way of life for Mongolians for thousands of years. Nomads are people who live a mobile lifestyle, moving from place to place in search of better grazing grounds for their livestock. They live in traditional tents called "gers" and follow a seasonal cycle of movements, taking their herds of horses, sheep, and cattle to new grazing grounds.

The traditional lifestyle of Mongolian nomads is centered around their livestock. They are skilled at raising and caring for their animals, which provide them with milk, meat, and wool. Nomads use every part of the animal, from meat for food to wool for clothing and tents. They also rely on their animals for transportation and as a source of income through the sale of livestock and animal products.

Nomads are also known for their hospitality and a strong sense of community. They welcome visitors with open arms and share their food and shelter without hesitation. The sense of community is particularly strong during festivals, such as the Naadam Festival, where nomads from different regions come together to celebrate and compete in traditional sports.

Despite the challenges of living a nomadic lifestyle, many Mongolians continue to choose this way of life. However, the lifestyle is not without its challenges, including harsh weather conditions, limited access to education and healthcare, and the threat of losing grazing lands due to modernization and urbanization.

In recent years, the Mongolian government has taken steps to support and preserve the nomadic way of life. They have created programs to provide education, healthcare, and other essential services to nomads, as well as to protect their grazing lands from development and industrialization.

❑

7.

The Silk Road

The Silk Road is an ancient network of trade routes that connected the East and the West, linking China to the Mediterranean world. The Silk Road played a crucial role in the economic, cultural, and political exchange between Asia and Europe.

The Silk Road was not a single road but rather a complex network of land and sea routes that extended over 7,000 miles. The road was named after the most valuable commodity traded along the route - silk. However, the Silk Road was not only a trade route for silk but also a conduit for the exchange of ideas, culture, and technology. The trade along the Silk Road included spices, textiles, precious stones, metals, and more.

Mongolia, located in the heart of Asia, played a critical role in the Silk Road trade. The country's location on the trade route made it a natural hub for trade and cultural exchange. Mongolian nomads were key players in the trade, as they provided transportation services for goods and travelers. The trade helped the Mongolians gain access to new technologies, goods, and ideas, which contributed to their cultural and economic development.

The Silk Road was also significant in terms of cultural exchange. The route allowed for the exchange of ideas, art, religion, and philosophy. Buddhism, for example, was introduced to Mongolia through the Silk Road. The influence of Buddhism can be seen in Mongolian art, architecture, and traditions.

However, the Silk Road was not without its challenges. The road passed through harsh environments, including deserts, mountains, and rivers. Merchants had to deal with bandits, extreme weather conditions, and political instability along the way. Despite these challenges, the Silk Road remained a vital trade route for over a thousand years.

Today, the Silk Road remains a symbol of cultural exchange and globalization. The route has inspired many modern-day initiatives, including the Belt and Road Initiative, which seeks to revive and expand the ancient Silk Road routes for modern-day trade and development.

❑

8.

Political Evolution

Mongolia has a rich history of political evolution that spans over centuries. From the ancient times of the Mongol Empire to the modern democratic government, Mongolia has undergone significant changes in its political landscape.

The Mongol Empire, founded by Genghis Khan in the 13th century, was one of the largest empires in history. The empire was ruled by the Khans, who were absolute monarchs. The empire's governance was based on a meritocracy system, where individuals were appointed based on their abilities rather than their social status. The empire's military prowess and sophisticated governance system contributed to its success.

After the collapse of the Mongol Empire, Mongolia was divided into several small states, each ruled by its own

Khan or feudal lord. In the 17th century, the Manchu Qing Dynasty of China conquered Mongolia and established a puppet government. The Qing dynasty ruled Mongolia until 1911 when Mongolia declared independence.

After gaining independence, Mongolia struggled to establish a stable political system. The country was under Soviet influence and adopted a communist government in 1924. The Mongolian People's Republic was established, and the country was ruled by the Mongolian People's Revolutionary Party (MPRP) until 1990.

In 1990, the democratic revolution took place in Mongolia, and the country transitioned from a one-party communist system to a multi-party democratic system. The MPRP renamed itself the Mongolian People's Democratic Party (MPDP) and transformed itself into a democratic socialist party. The country's first multi-party elections were held in 1992, and a new constitution was adopted in 1994.

Since then, Mongolia has continued to evolve politically. The country has held several democratic elections, and power has been peacefully transferred from one government to another. Mongolia is now a parliamentary republic, with a president as the head of state and a prime minister as the head of government.

Mongolia's political evolution has not been without challenges. The country faces issues such as corruption, poverty, and inequality. The government has been working to address these issues and improve the lives of its citizens. The country is also working to diversify its economy and reduce its reliance on mining, which has been a major contributor to its economy.

❑

9.

Mineral Resources

Mongolia is known for its vast mineral resources, which have played a significant role in its economy. The country is home to large deposits of copper, gold, coal, uranium, and other minerals.

Mining is a crucial sector of Mongolia's economy, and mineral resources contribute significantly to the country's GDP. The mining industry employs a significant portion of the country's workforce, and it is responsible for a substantial amount of foreign investment. The government has been working to attract more investment to the sector and to ensure that mining is conducted sustainably.

Copper is one of Mongolia's most significant mineral resources. The country's largest copper mine, Oyu Tolgoi, is located in the Gobi desert. The mine is jointly owned by the Mongolian government and Rio Tinto, a multinational mining company. The Oyu Tolgoi mine is expected to produce around 450,000 tonnes of copper per year, making it one of the largest copper mines in the world.

Gold is another mineral resource that is important to Mongolia's economy. The country has several large gold mines, including the Boroo Gold Mine and the Gatsuurt Gold Mine. The mining of gold has been a significant contributor to the country's GDP, and the government has been working to attract more investment to the sector.

Coal is also an essential mineral resource in Mongolia. The country has vast reserves of coal, and the mining of coal is a significant contributor to the country's economy. The Tavan Tolgoi coal mine is one of the largest coal mines in the world, and it is jointly owned by the Mongolian government and several international companies. The government has been working to develop the coal industry and to ensure that mining is conducted sustainably.

Uranium is another mineral resource that is significant to Mongolia's economy. The country has large deposits of uranium, and the mining of uranium has been a significant contributor to the country's GDP. The government has been working to develop the uranium industry and to ensure that mining is conducted sustainably.

Despite the significant economic benefits that come with mining, there are also environmental and social impacts.

Mining can have negative effects on the environment, including water pollution, soil erosion, and habitat destruction. The government has been working to ensure that mining is conducted sustainably and to minimize the negative impacts of mining on the environment.

❑

10.

Music and Dance

Mongolian music and dance have a rich history that dates back thousands of years. Traditional music and dance are an essential part of Mongolian culture, and they play a significant role in many festivals and ceremonies.

Mongolian music is unique and is characterized by its use of traditional instruments such as the morin khuur (horsehead fiddle), the yatga (zither), and the khoomii (throat singing). Throat singing is a unique style of singing in which the singer produces two or more distinct pitches simultaneously. This technique is often used in Mongolian music and is considered an essential part of Mongolian cultural heritage.

The morin khuur is a two-stringed bowed instrument and is one of the most important traditional instruments in Mongolia. It is often used in performances and is considered a symbol of Mongolian national identity. The yatga is a long zither with 13 to 21 strings that is played with a set of plucked strings, and it is commonly used in classical Mongolian music.

Dance is another important aspect of Mongolian culture. Traditional dances often depict scenes from everyday life, such as herding or hunting, and are accompanied by traditional music. The dances are usually performed in groups and are often characterized by the dancers' fluid movements and intricate footwork.

One of the most famous traditional dances in Mongolia is the "tsam dance." This dance is often performed during the Lunar New Year and other important festivals and is known for its colorful costumes and intricate choreography. The dance is often performed by Buddhist monks and is considered a religious ritual that symbolizes the triumph of good over evil.

In addition to traditional music and dance, Mongolia has also developed modern music genres such as pop and rock. These genres have gained popularity in Mongolia, particularly among younger generations. Mongolian pop and rock musicians often incorporate traditional instruments into their music, creating a unique blend of traditional and modern sounds.

Mongolian music and dance have played an essential role in preserving Mongolian cultural heritage. Through music and dance, Mongolians have passed down their traditions and stories from generation to generation. Traditional music and dance are also a source of national pride, and they are often used to celebrate important events and festivals.

❑

11.

National Parks and Reserves

Mongolia is home to some of the most spectacular landscapes and diverse wildlife on the planet. With its vast stretches of grasslands, deserts, and mountains, Mongolia has a unique and varied ecosystem that supports a range of plant and animal life.

Mongolia has a total of 29 protected areas, including four national parks, 13 nature reserves, and six strictly protected areas. The national parks and reserves cover an area of approximately 34 million hectares, which is roughly 13% of Mongolia's total land area. These protected areas are home to some of the rarest and most endangered species of flora and fauna in the world.

One of Mongolia's most famous national parks is the Gobi Gurvansaikhan National Park. Located in the southern part of the country, the park covers an area of

27,000 square kilometers and is home to the famous Khongoryn Els dunes, the largest dunes in Mongolia. The park is also home to a variety of wildlife, including the endangered snow leopard, ibex, and argali sheep.

Another popular national park is the Hustai National Park, which is located about 100 kilometers west of Ulaanbaatar, the capital of Mongolia. The park covers an area of 50,000 hectares and is known for its population of wild horses, known as takhi or Przewalski's horse. The takhi were once extinct in the wild, but thanks to the efforts of conservationists, they were reintroduced to Mongolia in the 1990s.

Mongolia's national parks and reserves are not only important for preserving the country's natural heritage, but they also play a vital role in supporting the livelihoods of local communities. Many of the parks are located in rural areas, and they provide employment opportunities for local people as park rangers, guides, and in other roles related to tourism.

❑

12.

The Desert and Its Wonders

Mongolia is known for its vast and diverse landscapes, from towering mountains to rolling grasslands. But perhaps one of the most fascinating and unique landscapes in Mongolia is its desert regions.

The Gobi Desert is the most famous and largest in Mongolia, covering an area of over 500,000 square kilometers. It is home to a variety of wildlife, including the elusive snow leopard, as well as camels, gazelles, and other desert-adapted species. The Gobi is also known for its stunning landscapes, including towering dunes, rocky cliffs, and ancient cave paintings.

One of the most popular attractions in the Gobi is the Flaming Cliffs, also known as Bayanzag. These cliffs are named for their vibrant red and orange colors, which are especially stunning at sunrise and sunset. The Flaming

Cliffs are also home to some of the most important dinosaur fossils ever discovered, including the first known velociraptor fossil.

Another fascinating desert region in Mongolia is the Khongoryn Els dunes. Located in the Gobi Gurvansaikhan National Park, these dunes are some of the largest in the world, reaching heights of up to 300 meters. The dunes are constantly shifting and changing shape, creating a dynamic and ever-changing landscape.

In addition to its stunning landscapes, Mongolia's deserts also hold cultural significance for the country's nomadic herders. Many of these herders have lived in the desert regions for centuries, adapting to the harsh and unpredictable environment. They rely on sparse vegetation and occasional water sources to sustain their livestock and way of life.

However, the desert regions of Mongolia also face several challenges, including desertification, climate change, and the impact of tourism. Desertification, or the process by which fertile land turns into desert, is a major issue in Mongolia, with over 70% of the country's land affected to some degree. This process is exacerbated by climate change, which is causing more frequent and severe droughts.

Tourism also has an impact on Mongolia's desert regions, with increased visitation leading to issues such as littering, erosion, and disruption of local wildlife. However, responsible tourism can also play a role in supporting the conservation of these regions and providing economic opportunities for local communities.

❑

13.

Ethnic Groups

Mongolia is a diverse country with a rich cultural heritage, and this is reflected in the wide range of ethnic groups that call it home.

The largest ethnic group in Mongolia is the Khalkh, who make up approximately 86% of the population. The Khalkh are predominantly Tibetan Buddhist and traditionally have been nomadic herders, moving with their livestock in search of grazing land. However, many Khalkh have now settled in urban areas, particularly in the capital city of Ulaanbaatar, and work in a variety of professions.

Another significant ethnic group in Mongolia is the Kazakh, who make up around 4% of the population. The Kazakh are predominantly Muslim and traditionally have been semi-nomadic herders, specializing in raising livestock such as horses, sheep, and goats. They have their own language and customs, which differ from those of the Khalkh and other ethnic groups in Mongolia.

The Buryats are another ethnic group in Mongolia, making up around 3% of the population. They are predominantly Tibetan Buddhist or shamanistic and traditionally have been nomadic herders, moving with their livestock across the steppes and mountains of Mongolia and neighboring Russia. They have their own language and unique customs, such as throat singing, which is a type of overtone singing that produces multiple notes simultaneously.

Other ethnic groups in Mongolia include the Dorvod, who are predominantly Muslim and traditionally have been herders and traders; the Tuvans, who are predominantly shamanistic and traditionally have been nomadic herders; and the Uriankhai, who are predominantly shamanistic or animistic and traditionally have been hunters and herders.

While each ethnic group in Mongolia has its own unique traditions and customs, many shared cultural practices unite them. For example, the Naadam festival, which takes place every July, is a national celebration that features traditional sports such as wrestling, archery, and horse racing and is attended by people from all over Mongolia.

Despite the diversity of its ethnic groups, Mongolia is a relatively homogenous society, with a strong sense of national identity. However, there have been some tensions between different ethnic groups, particularly in border regions, and efforts have been made to promote inter-ethnic harmony and understanding.

❑

14.

Modernization: Challenges and Progress

Mongolia is a country that has undergone rapid changes over the past few decades. Since the democratic revolution in 1990, the country has been pursuing a path of modernization and development, to become a prosperous and democratic nation. However, this process has not been without its challenges, and Mongolia has faced several obstacles on its path to modernization.

One of the primary challenges that Mongolia has faced in its modernization process is the need to balance economic development with environmental concerns. As a country with vast mineral resources, Mongolia has been eager to exploit its natural wealth to fuel its economic growth. However, this has often come at the expense of the environment, as mining operations have caused pollution, deforestation, and other environmental damage. In recent years, there has been growing recognition of the need to balance economic growth with environmental protection, and the government has taken steps to strengthen environmental regulations and promote sustainable development.

Another challenge that Mongolia has faced in its modernization process is the need to address social inequality. Although Mongolia has made significant progress in reducing poverty over the past few decades, there are still significant disparities in income and wealth between different groups in society. In particular, the gap between urban and rural areas remains large, with many rural communities still struggling with poverty and lack of access to basic services. The government has implemented several programs aimed at reducing poverty and improving social welfare, but more needs to be done to address these inequalities.

A related challenge is the need to improve access to education and healthcare. Although Mongolia has made significant progress in expanding access to these services over the past few decades, there are still significant disparities in access between different regions and socioeconomic groups. In particular, rural communities often lack access to quality healthcare and education, which can have serious consequences for their well-being and development. The government has implemented several programs aimed at improving access to healthcare and education, but more needs to be done to address these challenges.

Another key challenge facing Mongolia in its modernization process is the need to promote good governance and strengthen democratic institutions. Although Mongolia has made significant progress in this area since the democratic revolution in 1990, there are still concerns about corruption, political polarization, and other governance challenges. The government has implemented several reforms aimed at promoting transparency, accountability, and the rule of law, but more needs to be done to strengthen democratic institutions and promote good governance.

Despite these challenges, Mongolia has made significant progress in its modernization process over the past few decades. The country has experienced rapid economic growth, expanded access to education and healthcare, and made significant strides in reducing poverty. In addition, Mongolia has played an increasingly prominent role in regional and international affairs, forging closer ties with its neighbors and partners around the world.

❑

15.

Urbanization

Mongolia is a predominantly rural country with a nomadic tradition that has been present for centuries. However, the urbanization process began in the early 20th century with the establishment of the capital city, Ulaanbaatar. Over the years, the city has grown to become the political, economic, and cultural center of the country. In recent years, the urbanization process has accelerated, with a growing population moving from rural areas to cities in search of better opportunities.

Urbanization in Mongolia

The city of Ulaanbaatar was founded in 1639 as a nomadic trading center. In the 20th century, it grew in importance as Mongolia's political and economic center. In 1924, when Mongolia became a communist country,

Ulaanbaatar became the capital city. During this time, the government implemented several urbanization policies to transform the city from a nomadic trading center to a modern urban center. In the 1950s, several new buildings and infrastructure projects were built in the city, including the Ulaanbaatar Railway Station, the Central Stadium, and the State Department Store.

After the fall of communism in 1990, Mongolia transitioned to a market economy, leading to a surge in urbanization. The population of Ulaanbaatar grew rapidly, from around 500,000 in the 1990s to over 1.4 million today. The city's population now accounts for almost half of Mongolia's total population.

Current State of Urbanization

The rapid urbanization process in Mongolia has brought about many changes. It has led to the growth of Ulaanbaatar as a vibrant and dynamic city with a modern infrastructure and diverse population. However, the process has also brought about several challenges, such as increased pollution, inadequate housing, and urban sprawl.

The rapid growth of the city has put pressure on its infrastructure, particularly its transport and housing systems. The city's transport system, which includes a limited subway system and an extensive bus network, is often congested, leading to long commute times and high levels of pollution. Housing in the city is also inadequate, with many residents living in informal settlements with poor access to basic services such as water, sanitation, and healthcare.

Challenges and Opportunities

The rapid urbanization process in Mongolia presents both challenges and opportunities. One of the key challenges is the need to manage the growth of the city sustainably. This includes developing a modern and efficient transport system, improving housing conditions, and addressing environmental concerns such as air and water pollution.

However, urbanization also presents opportunities for economic growth and development. The growth of Ulaanbaatar has led to the development of new industries and businesses, such as finance, technology, and tourism. The city has become an important regional hub, attracting investment and providing a range of opportunities for its residents.

❑

16.

Renewable Energy

Mongolia is a country with vast, open spaces and a harsh climate that has traditionally relied on fossil fuels and traditional forms of energy. However, in recent years, Mongolia has been exploring the potential of renewable energy sources such as wind and solar power to diversify its energy mix and reduce its carbon footprint. This chapter will discuss the current state of renewable energy in Mongolia and the challenges and opportunities it faces.

Mongolia has abundant renewable energy resources, particularly in the form of wind and solar power. The country has some of the best wind resources in the world, with an estimated potential capacity of over 1,100 GW, more than ten times the country's current electricity demand. Similarly, Mongolia has some of the highest levels of solar radiation in Asia, making it an ideal location for solar power generation.

Despite this potential, renewable energy currently only accounts for a small percentage of Mongolia's energy mix. According to the Mongolian Ministry of Energy, in 2020, renewable energy sources accounted for just 8.6% of total electricity generation, with the majority still coming from coal-fired power plants. However, there are plans to increase this percentage in the coming years.

The Mongolian government has set ambitious targets for renewable energy generation, to reach 20% by 2023 and 30% by 2030. To achieve these targets, the government has implemented several policies and initiatives to support renewable energy development. For example, in 2017, the government launched the "Renewable Energy 2030" program, which aims to increase renewable energy capacity to 4 GW by 2030.

One of the challenges facing renewable energy development in Mongolia is the country's remote and dispersed population. Most of Mongolia's population is located in urban areas, while much of the country's renewable energy potential is in remote areas. This makes it challenging to build and maintain the necessary infrastructure to transmit renewable energy to where it is needed.

To address this issue, the Mongolian government has implemented several initiatives to support off-grid renewable energy solutions, particularly in rural areas. For example, the government has provided subsidies and other incentives for the installation of solar power systems in households and businesses that are not connected to the national grid.

Another challenge facing renewable energy development in Mongolia is the country's underdeveloped energy infrastructure. Mongolia currently has limited transmission and distribution networks, which can make it difficult to integrate renewable energy into the grid. The government is working to address this issue through initiatives such as the "Grid Reinforcement and Green Energy Corridor Project," which aims to develop the necessary infrastructure to support the integration of renewable energy into the grid.

❑

17.

Mongolian Cuisine

Mongolian cuisine is characterized by its simplicity, its reliance on meat and dairy products, and its strong ties to the country's nomadic culture. The harsh climate and limited access to ingredients have influenced the development of traditional Mongolian dishes. However, with the influx of tourists and increasing globalization, the food scene in Mongolia has undergone significant changes in recent years.

One of the most iconic dishes of Mongolia is undoubted "buuz," a steamed dumpling filled with ground meat, typically beef or mutton. These dumplings are often served with "suutei tsai," a salty milk tea made from black tea and milk. Other popular dishes include "khuushuur," a fried meat pastry, and "boodog," where a whole goat is cooked by placing hot stones inside its stomach cavity.

Mongolian cuisine is also heavily reliant on dairy products, particularly “airag,” a fermented mare’s milk that is slightly alcoholic. Other dairy products such as “urum,” a type of sour cream, and “aaruul,” dried curdled milk, are commonly used in dishes and snacks. “Tsagaan idee,” which is essentially milk rice pudding, is a popular dessert in Mongolia.

In recent years, the food scene in Mongolia has undergone significant changes due to the increasing urbanization and globalization. In Ulaanbaatar, the capital city, there is a growing number of international restaurants and cafes catering to locals and tourists alike. Mongolian chefs are also experimenting with fusion cuisine, combining traditional ingredients and flavors with international cooking techniques.

Despite these changes, traditional Mongolian cuisine remains an essential part of the country’s identity and culture. It is still prevalent in rural areas and among nomadic families who continue to rely on their livestock for sustenance. Many Mongolians take pride in their traditional cuisine and are eager to introduce visitors to their favorite dishes.

Regarding drinks, Mongolia has a long history of fermenting alcoholic beverages from milk, such as “airag,” “tarag,” and “shimiin arkhi.” Beer is also popular, with several local breweries producing their own versions. "Vodka" is also widely consumed, particularly during special occasions and celebrations.

❑

18.

Mongolian Equestrianism

Mongolian equestrianism is a traditional sport that has been practiced by the Mongol people for thousands of years. It is deeply rooted in their culture, and it reflects the strong bond between the Mongols and their horses. Mongolian equestrianism is one of the three "manly sports" that are still practiced today: wrestling, archery, and horse racing.

Horses have always played a critical role in Mongolian society. They are used for transportation, hunting, and warfare. The Mongol horse is known for its strength, endurance, and resilience, which makes it the perfect animal for the harsh Mongolian terrain. Moreover, the Mongol horse is an important part of Mongolian culture, and it is often celebrated in Mongolian art, music, and literature.

Mongolian equestrianism has several different forms, but perhaps the most famous is the horse race. The Mongolian horse race is a thrilling event that attracts thousands of spectators from all over the country. The races are usually held in the countryside, where the tracks can stretch for several miles. The horses are ridden by young jockeys, who are usually between the ages of six and thirteen. The jockeys ride without saddles, which makes the races even more challenging.

Another popular form of Mongolian equestrianism is the "khasaa," which is a type of polo. The game is played with a small wooden ball and long wooden sticks, and the objective is to score points by hitting the ball into the opposing team's goal. The game can be played on horseback or on foot, and it is often accompanied by music and dancing.

Mongolian equestrianism also includes various forms of horseback riding, such as "garid," which is a type of long-distance riding. The garid is a test of endurance and skill, as riders must navigate through rough terrain and harsh weather conditions.

In addition to being a sport, Mongolian equestrianism is also a way of life. Many Mongols still live as nomads, and horses play a critical role in their daily lives. For example, during the summer months, the nomads will often move their herds to new grazing areas. The horses carry the families and their belongings, and they are used to round up the sheep and goats. Without horses, it would be impossible for the nomads to survive in the harsh Mongolian environment.

Mongolian equestrianism has undergone some changes in recent years. Modern technology has made it easier to breed and train horses, and there are now more formalized training programs for young jockeys. However, the basic principles of Mongolian equestrianism remain the same. It is still a sport that celebrates the bond between the Mongols and their horses, and it is still an essential part of Mongolian culture.

❑

19.

Education System

Mongolia has undergone significant changes in its education system since the fall of communism in the early 1990s. The country has shifted towards a more open, democratic society with a renewed focus on education.

Educational Tradition

Mongolia has a rich educational tradition that dates back centuries. In ancient times, children learned the traditional way of life through oral traditions and apprenticeships. Later, during the rule of the Mongol Empire in the 13th and 14th centuries, education became more formalized, with schools established to teach reading, writing, and mathematics.

During the Soviet era, Mongolia's education system was modeled after that of the USSR, emphasizing Marxist-

Leninist ideology and the sciences. This led to a highly centralized and bureaucratic system, with a narrow focus on vocational and technical training rather than liberal arts education.

Current State

Since the transition to democracy in the 1990s, Mongolia has been working to modernize its education system. The government has implemented reforms aimed at improving the quality and accessibility of education at all levels, from preschool to university.

One major challenge facing Mongolia's education system is its limited resources. The country's vast, sparsely populated geography makes it difficult to provide equal access to education across all regions. Additionally, the lack of funding and infrastructure has resulted in poorly equipped schools and a shortage of qualified teachers, particularly in rural areas.

Despite these challenges, Mongolia has made significant progress in expanding access to education. In recent years, the government has invested heavily in building new schools and universities and has also implemented policies to improve the quality of teaching and curriculum. The country has also made strides in increasing enrollment in higher education, with over 60% of high school graduates now attending university.

Future Prospects

Moving forward, Mongolia's education system faces several key challenges. One is the need to address the persistent disparities in access to education between urban and rural areas. Another is the need to increase the quality of education at all levels, particularly in terms of critical thinking and problem-solving skills.

To address these challenges, the government has identified several key priorities for education reform. These include expanding access to early childhood education, improving the quality of teaching and curriculum, and promoting innovation and creativity in the classroom. Additionally, the government is working to strengthen partnerships between schools and local businesses, to better align education with the needs of the labor market.

❑

20.

Folklore and Literature

Mongolia is a country with a rich and diverse cultural heritage, and one of the key components of this heritage is its folklore and literature. Mongolian folklore is a blend of Shamanism, Buddhism, and Animism, which has evolved over centuries and reflects the country's nomadic lifestyle and traditions. Mongolian literature, on the other hand, has a relatively shorter history, but it still boasts some of the most significant works in the world of literature.

Mongolian Folklore

Mongolian folklore has a plethora of legends, myths, and stories. One of the most popular themes in Mongolian folklore is the story of the wolf, which is seen as a symbol of freedom, strength, and loyalty. According to the legend, the wolf was once a human who was transformed into a wolf due to his love for the wilderness. Other common themes in Mongolian folklore include the magical powers of shamans, the mysterious powers of nature, and the battle between good and evil.

One of the most significant elements of Mongolian folklore is the "Epic of King Gesar." The epic is a long poem that tells the story of a warrior king, Gesar, who was believed to have lived in the 11th century. The epic consists of 120 chapters, and it is one of the longest epic poems in the world. The poem has been passed down orally from generation to generation, and it is still recited by bards in Mongolia.

Mongolian Literature

Mongolian literature has a relatively shorter history compared to other world literature. The first known literary works in Mongolia date back to the 13th century when the Mongolian Empire was at its peak. Most of these works were written in the Mongolian script, which was created by Chinggis Khan to unify the various Mongolian tribes. The script is still used today, although it has undergone significant changes over time.

One of the most significant works in Mongolian literature is "The Secret History of the Mongols." The book is believed to have been written in the 13th century and is the oldest surviving literary work in Mongolian. The book chronicles the history of the Mongolian Empire from its origins to the reign of Chinggis Khan. It is a unique work of literature as it combines historical facts with myth and legend.

In the 20th century, Mongolian literature experienced a resurgence, and many significant works were written. One of the most notable works is “The Blue Sky,” written by Galsan Tschinag, a German-Mongolian writer. The book is a semi-autobiographical work that tells the story of a young Mongolian boy growing up in the Altai Mountains and his journey to becoming a writer.

❑

21.

Mongolian Fashion

Mongolia has a rich cultural heritage that is reflected in its clothing. Traditional Mongolian clothing is unique and reflects the nomadic lifestyle of the Mongolian people. However, with the influence of globalization and the changing times, Mongolian fashion has also evolved into modern styles.

Traditional Mongolian clothing is characterized by bright colors and bold patterns. The traditional dress for men is called a “deel,” which is a long robe that is usually made of silk or cotton. The deel has a high collar and long sleeves that taper at the wrist. The dress for women is also called a “deel,” but it is more fitted and has a broader skirt. The deel is usually made of silk or brocade and has a brightly colored sash that is tied around the waist.

Another traditional Mongolian garment is the “del” or fur coat, which is made from the pelts of animals such as sheep, goats, and camels. The del is usually lined with silk or cotton and has a hood to protect the wearer from the harsh Mongolian winter. The del is an essential garment for the nomadic lifestyle, as it provides warmth and protection against the elements.

Modern Mongolian fashion has embraced traditional elements while incorporating contemporary designs and materials. In recent years, Mongolian designers have gained international recognition for their innovative fashion designs. Many of these designers use traditional Mongolian fabrics such as silk and brocade in their designs, but they also incorporate modern materials such as leather and denim.

One example of modern Mongolian fashion is the brand “Mongol,” which was founded by designer Bayarmaa Bayarkhuu. The brand is known for its fusion of traditional Mongolian elements and modern designs. Mongol’s collections often feature brightly colored silk fabrics with intricate patterns, combined with contemporary silhouettes such as tailored blazers and cropped tros.

Another Mongolian fashion designer making waves in the industry is Tuguldur Batmunkh. Batmunkh’s designs are inspired by Mongolian history and culture, and he often incorporates traditional Mongolian motifs into his collections. His designs feature a blend of traditional Mongolian fabrics and modern materials such as leather and denim.

Mongolian fashion has also become popular among celebrities and fashion influencers. In 2018, the American rapper Kanye West visited Mongolia and was photographed wearing a traditional Mongolian deel. This sparked a trend among fashion enthusiasts, and traditional Mongolian clothing became a popular fashion statement.

In summary, Mongolian fashion is a unique blend of traditional and modern styles. Traditional Mongolian clothing reflects the nomadic lifestyle of the Mongolian people and is characterized by bright colors and bold patterns. Modern Mongolian fashion incorporates traditional elements while incorporating contemporary designs and materials. Mongolian designers are gaining international recognition for their innovative fashion designs, which are inspired by Mongolian history and culture. Mongolian fashion is a testament to the rich cultural heritage of the country and is a vibrant expression of its people.

❑

22.

Wildlife and Wilderness

Mongolia is a land of vast wilderness and diverse wildlife. Its unique landscape of rolling grasslands, high mountains, and vast deserts supports a wide range of animal species that are adapted to the harsh environment. From the snow leopard to the Gobi bear, Mongolia is home to some of the world's most endangered species.

The vast steppes of Mongolia support large herds of wild horses, gazelles, and antelopes. The wild horses of Mongolia, known as Przewalski's horses, are one of the most endangered equine species in the world. They were once extinct in the wild but have been reintroduced to the grasslands of Mongolia through conservation efforts. Mongolia is also home to the Mongolian gazelle, which is the most widespread of all the gazelle species. The

Mongolian gazelle is a vital prey species for the Mongolian wolf and snow leopard.

Mongolia's high mountains support a wide range of wildlife, including the iconic snow leopard. The snow leopard is one of the most elusive and endangered big cats in the world. It is estimated that there are fewer than 500 snow leopards left in Mongolia. The mountains of Mongolia are also home to the argali sheep, which is the largest wild sheep species in the world. The argali sheep are prized by hunters and are also an important prey species for the snow leopard.

The Gobi Desert is one of the harshest environments on Earth, but it is also home to some of the most unique wildlife. The Gobi bear, also known as the Gobi grizzly, is one of the rarest bear species in the world. There are only around 30 Gobi bears left in the wild, and they are found only in the Gobi Desert. The Gobi also supports a wide range of reptiles, including the Gobi viper, which is one of the most venomous snakes in the world.

Mongolia's wildlife is facing numerous threats, including habitat loss, poaching, and climate change. Overgrazing by livestock is also a significant problem, as it can lead to the loss of grasslands that support wildlife. Mongolia has made significant efforts to protect its wildlife through conservation programs and national parks. The creation of protected areas such as the Great Gobi Strictly Protected Area and the Hustai National Park has helped to preserve important habitats and protect endangered species.

The Mongolian government has also introduced laws to protect wildlife, such as the 1995 Law on Fauna, which prohibits the hunting of endangered species. However, enforcement of these laws can be a challenge due to limited resources and a lack of awareness among local communities.

In summary, Mongolia's wildlife and wilderness are an essential part of the country's natural heritage. Its unique landscape supports a diverse range of animal species that are adapted to the harsh environment. From the elusive snow leopard to the endangered Gobi bear, Mongolia's wildlife faces numerous threats but is also the subject of significant conservation efforts. Protecting Mongolia's wildlife and wilderness is not only important for the country's biodiversity but also for its cultural and economic significance.

❑

23.

Mongolia's Natural Beauty

Mongolia is a land of breathtaking natural beauty. From vast expanses of grasslands to soaring mountains and pristine lakes, the country's landscapes are diverse and awe-inspiring.

One of the most iconic landscapes in Mongolia is the vast grassland known as the steppe. This expansive terrain covers much of the country and is home to a wide variety of flora and fauna, including wild horses, gazelles, and numerous bird species. The steppe is also home to Mongolia's nomadic herders, who have lived and thrived in this landscape for centuries.

Mongolia is also home to several impressive mountain ranges, including the Altai Mountains in the west and the Khangai Mountains in the central part of the country. These towering peaks offer stunning views and are home to a diverse range of wildlife, including argali sheep, ibex, and snow leopards. The mountains also provide a wealth of recreational opportunities, including hiking, camping, and mountaineering.

Another natural wonder of Mongolia is its vast network of lakes and rivers. One of the most famous of these is Lake Khovsgol, a pristine alpine lake located in the north of the country. The lake is surrounded by snow-capped mountains and is home to a variety of fish species, including the taimen, one of the largest freshwater fish in the world. The lake is also a popular destination for boating, fishing, and swimming.

Mongolia is also home to several stunning national parks and protected areas. One of the most famous of these is Gorkhi-Terelj National Park, located just outside of the capital city of Ulaanbaatar. The park is home to a variety of wildlife, including brown bears, moose, and wolves, and offers a wealth of recreational activities, including hiking, horseback riding, and camping.

In addition to its stunning natural landscapes, Mongolia is also home to several unique geological formations, including the Flaming Cliffs of the Gobi Desert. These towering red cliffs are known for their rich deposits of dinosaur fossils, including those of the velociraptor, and are a popular destination for paleontologists and tourists alike.

In summary, Mongolia's natural beauty is a testament to the country's unique geography and rich cultural heritage. From its vast grasslands to its soaring mountains and pristine lakes, the country's landscapes offer a wealth of opportunities for exploration and adventure. As such, Mongolia's natural wonders are a true treasure and one that visitors to the country should be sure to experience for themselves.

❑

24.

Buddhism in Mongolia: Monasteries and Monks

Buddhism has played a significant role in the history and culture of Mongolia for centuries. The religion was introduced to Mongolia in the 16th century and has since become deeply ingrained in the country's traditions and way of life. In this chapter, we will explore the role of Buddhism in Mongolia, with a focus on its monasteries and monks.

Monasteries, or temples, are the most important institutions in the Mongolian Buddhist tradition. These monasteries are not only places of worship but also centers of learning, where monks receive an education in religious studies, philosophy, and the arts. Many of Mongolia's monasteries are located in remote and stunningly beautiful areas, making them not only spiritual sanctuaries but also important cultural landmarks.

One of the most famous monasteries in Mongolia is Gandantegchinlen Monastery, located in the capital city of Ulaanbaatar. This monastery was founded in 1838 and is home to over 150 monks. It is one of the few monasteries in Mongolia to have survived the religious purges of the 1930s and remains an important center of Buddhist learning and worship.

Another famous monastery in Mongolia is Erdene Zuu Monastery, located in the western city of Kharkhorin. This monastery was founded in 1585 and is considered to be the oldest surviving monastery in Mongolia. It is located on the site of the ancient capital of the Mongol Empire and is home to several important religious artifacts and artworks.

Monks are the spiritual leaders of the Mongolian Buddhist tradition. They are highly respected members of society and play an important role in the religious and cultural life of the country. Many monks live in monasteries and spend their days in meditation, prayer, and study. They also play an important role in the community, providing spiritual guidance and counseling to those in need.

One of the most famous monks in Mongolian history is Zanabazar, who lived in the 17th century. Zanabazar was not only a spiritual leader but also a renowned artist, who is credited with creating the Soyombo script, which is still used in Mongolia today. He was also a skilled sculptor, and many of his works can still be seen in museums and monasteries throughout the country.

In summary, Buddhism has played a significant role in the history and culture of Mongolia for centuries. Monasteries and monks are important institutions in the Mongolian Buddhist tradition, providing spiritual guidance, education, and cultural enrichment to the community. As such, they are a vital part of the country's heritage and a testament to the enduring power of the Buddhist faith.

❑

25.

Preserving the Environment

Preserving the environment has become an increasingly important issue in modern times, and Mongolia is no exception. The country's unique landscape and natural resources make it an important area for environmental protection, and in recent years, environmentalism has become an important movement in Mongolia. In this chapter, we will explore the role of environmentalism in Mongolia and the efforts being made to preserve the country's natural resources.

One of the most pressing environmental issues in Mongolia is desertification. Large areas of the country's grasslands are turning into deserts due to overgrazing, climate change, and mining activities. This has had a severe impact on the country's biodiversity, soil quality, and water resources. As a result, many environmental groups in Mongolia have focused their efforts on combatting desertification and restoring the country's grasslands.

One such group is the Mongolian Green Movement, which was founded in 1989 and has since become one of the most influential environmental organizations in the country. The group has focused its efforts on raising awareness about environmental issues, promoting sustainable development, and advocating for policies that protect the environment.

Another important environmental issue in Mongolia is air pollution. The country's capital city, Ulaanbaatar, is one of the most polluted cities in the world due to a combination of factors, including coal-burning stoves used for heating in the winter, traffic congestion, and industrial activities. This has had a severe impact on public health, with rates of respiratory diseases and other pollution-related illnesses on the rise.

To address this issue, the government of Mongolia has launched several initiatives to reduce air pollution, including promoting the use of cleaner fuels, improving public transportation, and providing subsidies for households to switch to cleaner heating options.

In addition to these efforts, there are also several grassroots environmental initiatives being undertaken in Mongolia. For example, the "Green Belt" movement aims to plant trees and other vegetation around the outskirts of Ulaanbaatar to improve air quality and combat desertification. There are also several initiatives aimed at promoting sustainable tourism and protecting Mongolia's unique wildlife, such as the snow leopard and the wild horse.

In summary, environmentalism has become an increasingly important movement in Mongolia, with many organizations and individuals working to preserve the country's natural resources. Desertification and air pollution are two of the most pressing environmental issues in the country, and efforts are being made at both the government and grassroots levels to address these problems. As the world becomes increasingly aware of the importance of environmental protection, environmentalism in Mongolia will likely continue to grow in strength and influence in the years to come.

❑

26.

The Legacy of Genghis Khan

The legacy of Genghis Khan has left an indelible mark on the world and continues to shape the course of history. Genghis Khan was the founder and first emperor of the Mongol Empire, which at its height spanned much of Asia, Eastern Europe, and parts of the Middle East. His legacy is multifaceted and complex, encompassing military conquest, cultural exchange, and the spread of new ideas and technologies.

One of the most significant legacies of Genghis Khan was his military prowess. Under his leadership, the Mongol army conquered vast territories and defeated some of the most powerful empires of the time. Genghis Khan's military strategy was based on mobility, speed, and surprise, and his troops were expert horsemen and archers. His victories paved the way for the expansion of the Mongol Empire and the establishment of a new world order.

Another important legacy of Genghis Khan was his role as a cultural mediator. The Mongols were nomadic people who had little exposure to the civilizations they conquered. However, Genghis Khan recognized the value of the knowledge and traditions of the conquered peoples and encouraged the exchange of ideas and technologies. As a result, the Mongols became a conduit for the spread of new ideas and technologies, including paper-making, gunpowder, and the compass.

Genghis Khan's legacy also includes the establishment of a new political and economic system. He created a centralized government with a strong military and a merit-based system of governance. This system allowed for the efficient administration of a vast and diverse empire and helped to ensure its stability and longevity. Genghis Khan also encouraged trade and commerce, which helped to stimulate the economy and promote cultural exchange.

Finally, Genghis Khan's legacy includes his influence on the development of the Mongolian language and culture. He was a great patron of the arts and encouraged the creation of new forms of literature, music, and dance. He also supported the development of a written script for the Mongolian language, which helped to promote literacy and education.

In summary, the legacy of Genghis Khan is a complex and multifaceted one that continues to shape the world today. His military conquests, cultural exchange, and contributions to politics and economics have left an indelible mark on history, and his influence on the development of the Mongolian language and culture is still felt today. As such, Genghis Khan remains one of the most influential figures in world history, and his legacy will continue to be studied and debated for generations to come.

❑

27.

The Future of Mongolia: Challenges and Opportunities

Mongolia is a country that is facing several challenges as it looks towards the future. However, it is also a country that is full of opportunities. In this chapter, we will explore some of the challenges and opportunities facing Mongolia and what the future might hold for this unique and fascinating country.

One of the biggest challenges facing Mongolia is economic development. While the country has made great strides in recent years, it still faces several obstacles in this area. For example, Mongolia's economy is heavily dependent on natural resources, such as coal, copper, and gold, and fluctuations in commodity prices can have a significant impact on the country's economic growth.

Another challenge facing Mongolia is its relatively small population and large land area. This can make it difficult to provide essential services to all areas of the country, and can also make it difficult to attract foreign investment. In addition, Mongolia's harsh climate and geography can make it a challenging place to live and work.

However, despite these challenges, Mongolia also has several opportunities for growth and development. For example, the country has a rich cultural heritage and a unique history that can be leveraged to attract tourists and promote cultural exchange. In addition, Mongolia has a wealth of natural resources that can be used to fuel economic growth, as long as these resources are managed sustainably.

Furthermore, Mongolia is strategically located between Russia and China, two of the world's largest economies. This puts Mongolia in a unique position to benefit from trade and investment from these countries. In addition, Mongolia has made significant strides in recent years in terms of political stability and democratization, which can help to attract foreign investment and improve the country's international standing.

To capitalize on these opportunities and address the challenges facing the country, there are several things that

Mongolia can do. For example, the country can continue to diversify its economy and reduce its reliance on natural resources by investing in other sectors such as tourism, technology, and manufacturing. Mongolia can also work to improve its infrastructure, including transportation and communication networks, to better connect the country and make it more accessible to investors and tourists.

Finally, Mongolia can continue to invest in education and human capital development, which can help to create a skilled and knowledgeable workforce that is capable of driving the country's economic growth and development.

In summary, while Mongolia faces several challenges as it looks toward the future, it also has a wealth of opportunities. By continuing to diversify its economy, improve its infrastructure, and invest in education and human capital development, Mongolia can position itself for success in the years to come. As the world continues to change and evolve, Mongolia has the potential to play an important role in the region and on the global stage.

❑

Epilogue

As we come to the end of the book "The rich culture and History of Mongolia", it is fitting to reflect on the richness and diversity of this fascinating country and its people. From the vast steppes to the rugged mountains, from the bustling cities to the serene countryside, Mongolia has a beauty and complexity that is both captivating and inspiring.

Throughout this book, we have explored many facets of Mongolian culture, history, and daily life. We have learned about the traditions and customs of the nomadic herders who have lived on the steppes for centuries, and about the challenges and opportunities facing Mongolia as it navigates the transition to a modern, urbanized society. We have marveled at the country's stunning natural landscapes, from the Gobi Desert to the taiga forests of the north, and learned about the unique plant and animal life that inhabit them.

One of the most striking aspects of Mongolian culture is its resilience and adaptability. Despite facing numerous challenges over the centuries, including invasions, political upheavals, and environmental pressures, the Mongolian people have maintained a strong sense of identity and pride in their traditions and heritage. This is evident in the enduring popularity of traditional arts such as music, dance, and handicrafts, as well as in the continued practice of nomadic herding, which remains the backbone of the country's rural economy.

At the same time, Mongolia is a country in transition, grappling with the complexities of modernization and globalization. Rapid urbanization, driven by a booming mining industry and a growing middle class, is transforming the country's social and economic landscape, bringing both new opportunities and new challenges. The government is working to balance economic growth with environmental sustainability, while also promoting social inclusion and human rights.

As we look to the future, it is clear that Mongolia has much to offer the world. Its rich cultural heritage, stunning natural beauty, and unique traditions and customs make it a fascinating and rewarding destination for travelers and scholars alike. At the same time, its strategic location between China and Russia, coupled with its abundant natural resources and growing economy, make it an important player in regional and global affairs.

As we conclude this book, we hope that readers will come away with a deeper appreciation and understanding of this remarkable country and its people. We also hope that this book will inspire further exploration and study of Mongolian culture, history, and society, and contribute to a greater appreciation of the richness and diversity of human experience.

❑

Printed in the USA
CPSIA information can be obtained
at www.ICGtesting.com
LVHW041115191023
761449LV00010B/1365